John Russell Bartlett

The Barbarities of the Rebels

As Shown in their Cruelty to the Federal Wounded and Prisoners

John Russell Bartlett

The Barbarities of the Rebels
As Shown in their Cruelty to the Federal Wounded and Prisoners

ISBN/EAN: 9783744755085

Printed in Europe, USA, Canada, Australia, Japan

Cover: Foto ©ninafisch / pixelio.de

More available books at **www.hansebooks.com**

THE

BARBARITIES OF THE REBELS,

AS SHOWN IN THEIR

CRUELTY TO THE FEDERAL WOUNDED AND PRISONERS; IN
THEIR OUTRAGES UPON UNION MEN; IN THE MUR-
DER OF NEGROES, AND IN THEIR UNMAN-
LY CONDUCT THROUGHOUT
THE REBELLION.

BY COLONEL PERCY HOWARD,

LATE OF THE ROYAL HORSE GUARDS.

PROVIDENCE, R. I.
PRINTED FOR THE AUTHOR.
1863.

PREFACE.

The compiler of this pamphlet, who has seen much military service in the wars of Asia and Europe, has, in common with the friends of humanity and civilization throughout the world, watched with the deepest interest the progress of the American rebellion. He, too, alike with all who hear and read of the progress of events in this unnatural war, has been shocked with the barbarities with which the war has been conducted by the South; barbarities which no war of ancient or modern times has exhibited, and which the savages of America, Africa or Polynesia never approached. These cruelties, inflicted by the Confederates upon Federal prisoners, upon Union men who would not uphold treason, and upon inoffensive negroes, ought to be made known, particularly to those in Great Britain who sympathize with the rebellious States ; who are aiding them to maintain their independence, and in the establishing of an empire " whose foundations," to use the words of Vice President Stephens " are based upon slavery." The unmanly acts of the rebel government and many of its military officers, which none but barbarians would resort to, deserve also to be made known.

With this view the compiler has cut from the newspapers and from official reports the accounts here presented, the authority for all of which is given. He believes that the facts here presented should be read by the soldiers in the Federal armies; by the " Copperheads " who sympathize with the rebels, and would make peace with them on their own terms, and by Europeans generally.

INDEX.

A RECORD

OF THE

BARBARITIES OF THE REBELS.

BARBARITIES OF THE TEXANS.

A correspondent of the Boston *Traveller*, writing from New Orleans, gives details of most horrid barbarities committed upon Union men, that the human mind can conceive of. The most terrible cruelties inflicted by savages, are mild to those of the barbarous Texans. The letter referred to, is filled with minute details of individual suffering, wherein cruelty, treachery, and cold-blooded murder are combined to an extent that the mind is filled with horror at the perusal of such barbarities. Among these is the case of Mr. James, who was travelling through Texas, from California. One day he was seen talking with some negroes, when he was charged with being a Yankee abolitionist, endeavoring to entice the negroes to run away. The man was hung in the town of Orange, on which occasion, Dr. Huson, a physician of the place, was particularly active, " mutilating the dead body, and while so doing, giving vent to the most horrid sentiments."

" Dr. Huson cut out the heart and placed it in a glass pickle jar filled with Louisiana whiskey, and this murdered man's heart has been seen by various persons since his execution, and it can be seen to-day in the drug and paint store of Dr. Huson, in the town of Orange. After this they actually tried out all the fat from the flesh and divided it among each other for the oiling of their firearms. One of the doctors, not Huson, secured the head and carried it home, telling his wife to boil it until all the flesh should drop off. Mr. Plummer could not at the moment recollect this brutal doctor's name, but the wife refused to have anything to do with the head, and was horror-struck at the barbarous sight. Her husband compelled her to place the skull in a large copper kettle and boil it for several hours, when he took charge of it, told his wife he had long desired an Abolitionist's skull for his study, and now he had got one.

1

Charles Saxon, a most inhuman man and daring robber, gave a ball, a week or two after the murder, in honor of the Vigilance Committee, whose business was to clean out all anti-slavery people from Texas. He invited all the secesh of Orange, of both sexes, to the ball, and as an inducement to attend the assembly he told them he should exhibit a genuine ' Yankee ' skull. He had borrowed the skull from the doctor, and fastening it to a shelf, placed a candle in each eye-socket, and while most of the guests looked on with exultation and satisfaction to behold the Yankee head, he made the remark that 'Yankee candlesticks were a decided improvement over the old-fashioned ones.'

"Females," the writter adds, "mingled in this wicked and horrible orgie." The letter referred to, was reprinted in the New York *Tribune*, Feb. —, 1863, where the details fill two columns.

MURDER OF TWO THOUSAND NEGROES BY TEXANS, AT BRASHEAR CITY.

The following is an extract from a letter from New Orleans, published in the New York *Tribune*, June 30, 1863 :

" I regret that I have to come to you with a record of cruelties, the like of which challenges history for a comparison. A week ago, Brashear City was surprised and captured, with all the troops, numbering about 1,000 men, including nearly all the Ironsides Regiment. Major Morgan, three or four officers, and about 150 men, being absent from the regiment at the time, are the only ones who are free. Before I come to my story of cruelties, I express what is every day being repeated by all hands, that the surprise was the most disgraceful and inexcusable of almost any in the history of the war.

Now, my story : From two men who escaped, and from rebel sympathizers in the city, I learn that the great contraband camp near Brashear City was dashed upon by the furious Texans. When in the camp a few weeks previously, I found there as many as 6,000 old men, women, and children. Of these, 2,000 or 3,000 were removed before the attack. Those who remained were slaughtered by the Texan cavalry in the most shocking manner. The cry of the sucking babe, the prayer of the aged, the shrieks of the mother, had no effect. The slaughter was terrible. I thought the massacre at St. Martinsville, where 500 men were found on mules striving to reach Gen. Banks' army, and were surrounded, captured, and all hung—I thought that, of a month ago, was bad enough ; but this eclipses it completely.

One incident about a few black soldiers at the surprise at Brashear. Capt. Allen, one of Gen. Ullman's recruiting officers, had about 150 recruits, with a couple of recruiting sergeants. They were all armed, and on board a car, waiting patiently to start for New Orleans in a few moments. The attack was made. The captain was not surprised. He and his men made a breastwork of the car, and there they fought the rebels alone, *till nearly every one died.* Those who survived were instantly slain by the ruffians, who hungered for their blood as a lion for his prey. Whether the captain survived is a mystery. When, Oh ! when shall the nation rise to a comprehension of the infamous character of the wretches who thus, in the face of heaven and earth, and in the boasted light of this nineteenth century, perpetrate these attrocities within our borders? God enable all our loyal men and women to discard, despise, and disown any who talk of ' peace ' with such wretches.''

MASSACRE OF GERMANS IN TEXAS.

The following article is a translation from *The Galveston Union*, a German paper, established since the occupation of that place by the Union forces. It will prove an incentive to still higher deeds of loyalty and heroism by the Germans now doing service in the ranks of the Union army, and may be read with profit by those rebel sympathizers who are opposed to the Government bringing the whole South to allegiance.

" Near the origin of the Gaud Cape and Piedruales, on Johnston's Creek, several American and two German families settled but two years ago. Contending against the roughness of the soil and the wild Indians, they had no pleasant position, but they persevered, conscious of their courage and their intrepidity, and the lower settlements owed it to them that they had less to suffer from the raids of the Indians. These border inhabitants received but little news about the condition of the country and the events of the war. All at once they were notified to pay war taxes and to drill. The first demand they could not comply with, because they had no money, not even corn meal for their families ; and the last orders they could not obey because they lived so distant from each other, and their absence would leave their familes without protection.

For these reasons they were considered Union men, and Capt. Duff, a notorious rowdy, was sent against the settlers with a company of Texans. They asked the protection of their friends, but had to fly from the overpowering numbers of their enemies to the mountains. Many Germans and Americans were arrested and imprisoned in Fredericksburg, and Capt. Duff was reinforced by 400 men, to operate successfully against the German abolitionists, and hunt up the Yankees. The soldiers again visited Johnston's Creek, but found the most of the settlers had fled to the mountains. Frederick Degener alone they surprised, sleeping under the porch of his house; but awakened by the cries of distress of his wife and the discharge of muskets of his enemies, who fired fourteen shots after him, he fortunately made his escape.

His house was ransacked and all movable property taken off. Other farms in the neighborhood were also searched, the farmers taken prisoners, and the houses burnt down. Upon the news of these events, Frederick Degener and other fugitives concluded to fly to Mexico. More exiles joined them, and soon they had a company of sixty-eight men. But they travelled too slowly, and before daybreak, one morning, they were surprised by 200 Texans. After a most determined resistance, they were defeated, and only twelve of them, covered with wounds, made good their escape.

All fugitives which afterwards fell into the hands of the enemy were hung up. Among these sixty-eight men only five were Americans, the others all Germans. A few of the fugitives escaped across the Rio Grande; others, wandering in the mountains and suffering extreme hunger, sought protection among American families, but were handed over to their persecutors and shot or hung.

To this news, Dr. Adolph Deuai, a celebrated German traveler, who for many years had lived in that country, makes the following notes:

'We know personally the most of these unfortunate victims, who have been murdered so mercilessly—not because they rebelled against the Government, but because they would not act against the Union, and would rather fly to Mexico. These murdered Union men were some of the greatest benefactors of the State. They had done the hardest pioneer work in it; cleared it from the wild beasts and Indians; they had saved it to civilization through more than one period of pestilence and famine; secured as borderers their present persecutors, the slaveholders, against the invasions of Indians, and done the best service as volunteers in the Mexican war and the wars on the frontier. They placed the arts and sciences in Texas as well as they could be found anywhere among the American Germans. They furnished the proof that they could cultivate sugar and cotton without the least danger to health, and increased the riches of the country millions of dollars.'

The above related events are their reward for it. Hundreds who succeeded in making their escape rove about in the woods, having lost everything, some even their families. Hundreds are now chased like wild beasts through the wilderness of Northwestern Texas, and succumb because of the most horrid tortures, their fate never being known to their fellow men."

WHOLESALE PERSECUTION OF UNION MEN IN TEXAS.

If anything were needed to show the Government the importance of hastening the movement for the occupation of Texas, the reports of the horrid atrocities constantly perpetrated by the rebels upon the Union citizens of that State supply conclusive testimony on the point, and present, besides, motives for immediate action which it would be inhuman not to respect. Among the many notices furnished by correspondents of the butcheries committed by the rebels, the following, recorded by a correspondent of the *Boston Traveller*, is one of the latest and most revolting:

"Several months since the Union sentiment cropped out so strongly in the counties of Kendall, Kimball, Gillispee and Kerr that they were declared to be in a state of rebellion against the Confederate Government, and a force of five hundred armed men, under one J. M. Duff, was sent into the several counties to crush out the Unionists, and confiscate the property of every man who refused to take the oath of allegiance within ten days.

"Duff commenced his bloody work by instructing his minions not to take prisoner any man found away from his family. In one day he hung sixteen Union men, and some time after the bodies of five others were dragged out of a water hole in a creek near Fredericksburg, each with a stone fastened about his neck. Duff, the leader of the expedition, has been promoted for 'gallant services.' "

A BAPTIST PREACHER SHOT.

The same correspondent narrates the following :

"In Blanco county recently, a native of Mississippi, who, though a slaveholder, was a Union man, was accused of being an abolitionist. He shot his accuser, and in company with his brother escaped on horseback, leaving his family at the mercy of the rebels. A Baptist preacher, also a slaveholder, named Elliott, who chanced to be at the house of the Union-ist a few days previous to the shooting affair, was arrested on State authority, on suspicion of being in sympathy with him and aiding him to escape. He was partially examined, but nothing being proved against him, he was re-manded to the custody of the Provost Marshal for further examination at a future day. On his way to prison he was seized by an infuriated mob and hung."

A MAZEPPA-LIKE ESCAPE.

" Your readers are familiar with the escape of General A. J. Hamilton from Texas, but the General himself may still be ignorant of the fate of one of his companions, Clum McKane, whose adventures find no parallel save in the tragic play of Mazeppa. When Hamilton escaped from Texas a reward of one thousand dollars was offered for his arrest, and he was pursued by a party of Texan rangers, who followed him into Mexico, and while dogging his path in the rear, they sent messengers ahead, who report-ed to the rancheros that the General and his companions were a band of thieves.

" Finding it impossible to obtain food on the road, Hamilton dispatched Clum to Camargo for a permit to travel. He was taken prisoner by the rebels, stripped naked and bound to a high spirited horse, which was let loose among the chapparal. The poor fellow was thus borne several miles, the thorns and points of the prickly pear lacerating his body in a shocking manner. Weak and bleeding, he was taken across the Rio Grand to San Ignacio, to be hung. A handkerchief which his would-be murderers had stolen from him was returned as he was entering the town, and this tied about his loins constituted his only covering.

" A relative of his wife interceded and saved his life, and he was taken to San Antonio and thrown into prison, where he remained several months with a ball and chain attached to his limbs. Finally, however, through the efforts of the Governor of New Leon, he was released.

RESISTANCE TO CONSCRIPTION.

" Since Magruder took command of the Confederate forces in Texas, the work of conscription has been prosecuted with relentless severity.

All who could not purchase exemption have been forced into the rebel army. In one county — San Patricio, containing nine hundred square miles — only twelve men are left at home, all the others having been taken for soldiers, either by draft or conscription. The result is that none are left to cultivate the soil, and the sufferings among the families of these men are heart-rending. With flour at one hundred and twenty dollars a barrel, and corn at twenty-five dollars per bushel, what chance for existence is there for the wife and children of a soldier whose pay is from eleven to thirteen dollars per month? Starvation stares the people in the face, and unless the strong arm of the Federal government interposes in their behalf, and that, too, right speedily, Texas will become a land of famine-stricken widows and orphans. But the people do not submit tamely to the despotic sway of Magruder. In Fayette and the adjoining counties between six and seven hundred men have organized to resist the conscription."

DEPRECIATION OF CONFEDERATE CURRENCY PUNISHABLE WITH DEATH.

"One of the most heinous of crimes of which a man can be guilty in Texas, is speculating in Confederate currency, which is held to be so sacred that the slightest attempt to depreciate its value is punished with death. Here is a case in point. A man living on the Salou river, near San Antonio, was asked if he had steers to sell. He replied in the affirmative, but added that he preferred not to sell them for paper money. The next day two men, well dressed and of gentlemanly deportment, drove up to his house in a carriage, and with an air of the utmost friendship, inquired the way to some point. The farmer came out to give the desired information, when he was seized, forced into the carriage, and without permitting the poor man to bid his family farewell, they hurried him away. Two days after, his agonized children, wondering at his long absence, started out in pursuit of him, when they were horrified at finding his lifeless body suspended to a tree. A venerable man, named Nelson, whose head was silvered over with the frost of nearly seventy winters, and who had amassed a snug property, believing that the Union of all the States would best conduce to the interests of each, was hung, his wife being compelled to witness his murder, and then, as if to leave no habitation in which the ghost of a Unionist might dwell, the murderer burned down the house."

HANGING SIXTEEN UNION MEN IN KENTUCKY.

Sixteen loyal Kentuckians were hung by the rebels about three weeks age, near the Cumberland Gap. Most of them belonged to Lincoln County, and were captured by a Tennessee regiment attached to Kirby Smith's command. Harper King, who lived within three miles of Crab Orchard, organized a company for Col. Bramlite's regiment, but afterwards resigned on account of ill health. But after Morgan's entrance into the State, the life of King was in constant danger. His house was burned, his horses stolen, and all his available property confiscated by Morgan and his gang. King and twenty-six of his friends formed themselves into a company for mutual protection, and lived in the woods. They all succeeded in procuring arms and ammunition from the Union men, and eluded the pursuit of the guerillas during the entire reign of their chief.

About this time the larger part of a regiment was made up for Kirby Smith's army, and the judge of Lincoln county court was made the lieutenant colonel. Of course, King and his men were known by this rebel colonel and many of his men. On the retreat of Bragg's army, around which all the little rebel squads gathered to make their final exit from Kentucky, these twenty-six loyal exiles, with their gallant leader, were surprised and surrounded by a Tennessee regiment. Some succeeded in escaping through the brush, but King and twelve of his men were captured. They were taken to headquarters, and by the advice of this rebel judge and lieutenant colonel, were condemned as bushwackers. The day of their execution was put off until they should get into a safer position, for Gen. Buell's advance was in sight of Bragg's rear, when those thirteen were captured.

They moved on as rapidly as possible to the gap, and on arriving there, these men, with six others, were tried as bushwackers, and sixteen condemned.

King declared he would not be hung, and maintained it to the last. His two sons, who belonged to his party, were hung up before him, and all the others, so as to exasperate him to the last degree. In the midst of all he stood firm, and when it came to his turn, he would not suffer the rope to be adjusted to his neck. They then knocked him on the head and then hung him. Another brother of King, fearing the execution of his brother, went to the gap, but arrived too late to see him alive. They had buried them all in a common trench.

He and his friends, on their way home, with the disinterred bodies of

King and his two sons, came across three rebel soldiers, sick and at a Union hospital, and hung them to a sycamore tree on the banks of the Rockcastle River. The deaths of more by hanging will follow.—*Cincinnati Commercial.*

These statements are corroborated by a letter from Mount Vernon, an extract from which was published in the New York *Tribune.* The particulars of the hanging of Capt. King and others of his company are given. It was a regularly organized company, raised for the protection of Crab Orchard. The execution was ordered by General Bragg.

HANGING UNION MEN IN TENNESSEE.

A correspondent of the *Nashville Union,* writes from our army in Southeastern Tennessee thus:

"The barbarity of the bushwackers is unexampled. About ten days ago our scouts found the bodies of four Union soldiers hanging to one tree. They appeared to have been hanging for two or three days.

"A few days since, while I was out with a scouting party, we found the body of a well dressed young lady, shot through the breast!

"We discovered that she belonged to a respectable family, two miles distant, every member of which had been murdered. She had evidently been shot while trying to escape.

"I had partaken of the hospitality of her father's table but three days before; and as I kneeled by her side, and felt no pulse, no breath, no sign, I could but think of my sister, of my mother, of my friend.

"Oh God! that flesh and blood should be cheap.

"We buried her there, among the rocks and pines of the mountain, and seven of Ohio's sons vowed by her grave that her death should be avenged."

REBEL BARBARITIES IN MISSOURI.

The following official report describes rebel barbarities:

"HEADQUARTERS FIFTH CAVALRY, MISSOURI STATE MILITIA, }
    INDEPENDENCE, Mo., January 11, 1863. }

"GENERAL:—Private Johnson, of the artillery company, was brought in dead to day. He is the fifth one murdered last week, four from the artillery and one from the militia. If you could see their mangled bodies you would not wonder why it is that I write you that guerrillas' wives should be forced out of the country. They were all wounded, and killed afterward, in the most horrible manner that fiends could devise; all were shot in the head, and several of their faces are terribly cut to pieces with boot heels. Powder was exploded in one man's ear, and both ears cut off close to his head. Whether this inhuman act was committed while he was alive or not, I have no means of knowing. To see human beings treated as my men have been by outlaws, is more than I can bear.

" Ten of these men, armed as they are, with their wives and children to act as spies, are equal to twenty-five of mine. Guerrillas are threatening Union women in the county. I am arresting the wives and sisters of some of the most notorious ones, to prevent them from carrying their threats into execution. They have also levied an assessment upon the loyal men of the county, and are collecting it very fast. There are many complaints on the subject, as some of those assessed claim to be Southern sympathizers. Some of the Union men have asked me if the order suspending your assessments applies to the one spoken of above. I tell them I do not know—to ask J. Brown Hovey.

" Yours truly,
" W. R. PENICE,
" Colonel Fifth Cavalry, M. S. M.

" General Ben. Loan, Jefferson City, Mo."

A Brookfield (Mo.) correspondent of the St. Louis *Democrat* furnishes the following :

" A cold-blooded murder was committed in Miami, Saline county, Missouri, on Thursday, the 18th of June, of which as yet no correct account has appeared in print.

" Mr. Daniel De Shella, who was in the early part of the present war, a commissioned officer in a company of independent scouts under Sigel, and was discharged on the expiration of his term of service, has since then (until the last six months) been co-operating with General Loan and others, in every way that intellectual energy and patriotism could devise to forward the interests of the Union and punish treason, thereby rendering himself obnoxious to traitors and copperheads, and their emissaries, the bushwackers.

" On the 18th, Mr. De Shella was followed from Petite Saw Plains to

Miami by a party of from twenty to twenty-four men, and probably would have been shot before reaching the town had he not been riding with ladies. He left them on entering the town to go into the post office, when he saw the band approaching, and as they wore the federal uniform he went towards them, but recognizing some of them as rebels, he guessed their errand, and being unarmed, returned to the post office, and asked the postmaster what to do. The postmaster told him to stay where he was. He replied that he would never be taken alive. He was then shown a back door through which he attempted to escape. But the rebels missing him, sent two mounted men to intercept him, which they did, and immediately fired on him, causing him to fall. They then demanded his surrender. He said, ' Never! never!' Upon which they rode closer to him and shot him six times through the head and breast ; any one of the shots would have been fatal. When they rejoined the band, they remarked that they ' had left him in hell with Lyons.'

" This version of the affair was given by one of the rebels. The following night the same party attacked the house of William Rennick, of Petite Saw Plains, a Union man who had been in the service, and whose son is now in a Missouri regiment. There were five men, two young ladies, daughters of Mr. Rennick, and some children in the house. The girls and children asked the attacking party to let them go from the house to a place of safety. They were told with oaths to send the men out or they would all be burned together. The house was set on fire, but the night being damp, the house would not burn. There were but two rifles in the house, and with these two the five men repulsed twenty-five. No one in the house was injured, although the house was perforated with bullets."

THE CARNIVAL OF MURDER.

There are at this day not less than twenty thousand officers in the Union armies exposed not merely to the hardships, perils and sufferings of war, but to the superadded horrors of cold-blooded murder. Any causal surprise or ambush, any disabling wound which stretches one of them on the ground in the path of an advancing rebel force, subjects him to the penalty of a felon's death. Let us present more conspicuously the passages in Mr. Jeff. Davis's Message, of the 12th inst., wherein that penalty is threatened :

" The public journals of the North have been received, containing a proclamation, dated on the first day of the present month, signed by the President of the United States, in which he orders and declares all slaves within ten of the States of the Confederacy to be free, except such as are found within certain districts now occupied in part by the armed forces of the enemy. We may well leave it to the instincts of that common humanity which a beneficent Creator has implanted in the breasts of our fellow-men of all countries, to pass judgment on a measure, by which several millions of human beings of an inferior race—peaceful and contented laborers in their sphere—are doomed to extermination, while at the same time they are encouraged to a general assassination of their masters by the insidious recommendation ' to abstain from violence unless in necessary self-defence.' *Our own detestation of those who have attempted the most execrable measure recorded in the history of guilty man is tempered by profound contempt for the impotent rage which it discloses.* So far as regards the action of this Government on such criminals as may attempt its execution, I confine myself to informing you that I shall—unless in your wisdom you deem some other course more expedient—*deliver to the several State authorities all commissioned officers of the United States that may hereafter be captured by our forces in any of the States embraced in the proclamation, that they may be dealt with in accordance with the laws of those States providing for the punishment of criminals engaged in exciting servile insurrection.* The enlisted soldiers I shall continue to treat as unwilling instruments in the commission of these crimes, and shall direct their discharge and return to their homes on the proper and usual parole."

In point of fact, a great majority of the "enlisted soldiers" heartily approve and indorse the President's proclamation of freedom—a far larger proportion of them than of their officers. But neither class is in the least degree responsible for that most righteous and salutary act of the President, as Davis well knows. And neither will ask any mercy at his hands.

Jeff. proposes to murder all Union officers because his "detestation" of the Proclamation of Freedom is "tempered by profound contempt." But for this, he would probably have ordered our soldiers as well as officers to be roasted alive—that being the discipline often accorded to inciters of slave insurrections.

President Lincoln proclaims the freedom of the slaves of rebels. Jeff. declares that this dooms "several millions" of "peaceful and *contented* laborers" to "extermination." By whom? Where? How? *We*, certainly, shall not so treat them ; and if they are indeed "peaceful and contented," why should Jeff. ? And if no servile insurrection is incited by our officers, nor even attempted, what are they to be murdered for? Suppose an attempt to convict them under "the laws of these States provided for the punishment of criminals," what evidence of criminal attempt or act on their part is to justify a jury in finding a verdict of Guilty?"—*New York Post.*

There is no doubt that the blood-thirsty Davis intended carrying out his threat, and several officers of the Union army who had been taken prisoners, were transferred, in conformity with the order of the rebel President, to the authorities of the State in which they were captured. The intention of the Governors of these States was to try these officers for inciting an insurrection among the slaves, and punish them in accordance with their laws for that offence, which is death. To what extent this brutal order of Davis was carried out we are in ignorance. The names of several U. S. officers who were captured in Alabama were announced in the Southern papers as being condemned to suffer death; but we are of opinion that the large number of rebel officers who fell into our hands, immediately after, alone deterred Davis and the rebel governors for carrying out their threat.

PERSECUTION OF LOYALISTS OR UNION MEN. HORRORS OF DAVIS'S CONSCRIPTION.

The *Chicago Tribune* contains a letter from Memphis, Mississippi, dated Feb. 11, 1863, giving an account of the frightful atrocities committed by the officers sent by Davis to enforce the conscription act in East Tennessee, Northern Alabama and Mississippi. In the first named district, the loyal men are numerous. Many of these escaped through the mountains to Kentucky, where they joined the Union army. In Alabama and Mississippi the poor creatures are too distant from the Union lines to make their escape. "Here," says the writer, "the most perfect reign of terror the world ever saw is now experienced by the unfortunate residents. In Mississippi, not satisfied with the conscription act of the Confederate Congress, which compelled all men from 18 to 40 to serve in the army, the legislature of that State has recently enacted a law extending the act to all from 40 to 60 years of age. The more thoroughly to enforce this law, Mississippi has been laid off into districts, twenty miles square, and a recruiting Colonel appointed for each district.

"In Northern Alabama," continues the writer, "it is even worse,

There are many Union men in that section of the State, and the minions of Jeff. Davis are busy in their efforts to force them into the Confederate ranks. The Union men have lain hid out in woods and caves rather than be taken as conscripts. This induced a novel hunt for them, and guerrillas and blood-hounds have been put upon their track, and many a poor victim has been smelled out in this way. Not long since, a young girl, carrying food to her father who was hiding in a cave, was attacked by one of these blood-hounds and torn to pieces.

"It is estimated that not less than 1,000 Union men from Mississippi and Alabama have made their way to Corinth, where Gen. Dodge made all possible provision for them.

"Gen. Dodge sent out and brought in the families of persecuted and downtrodden Union men, and has thus established a sort of encampment or home for all their families at Purdy, where they are likely to be free from persecution.

"Among those who recently suffered persecutions are the following: Abraham Kennedy and J. A. Mitchell, of Hacketboro Settlement, in Monroe county, Ala., have been hung by the rebels for indulging in Union proclivities. Mr. Hall, wife and daughter, of the same county, have been shot, and the latter killed. Peter Lewis, who was by his immediate neighbors suspected of Union proclivities, was hunted down by blood-hounds, and captured. The houses of J. A. Palmer, Wesley Williams and other Union men, were burned over their families' heads, and the people in the neighborhood notified that if they harbored them, their own houses would be burned. Mr. Peterson, living at the head of Bull Mountain, was killed for Union sentiments. Two women in Ilawimbia county were torn to pieces by blood-hounds.

"In addition to the foregoing, hundreds of families have been driven out of Alabama, and have reached Corinth on foot, without food or clothing. Some of them are old men, eighty years of age."

ILL TREATMENT OF GOVERNOR JOHNSON'S FAMILY.

Parson Brownlow writes from Cincinnati to the Philadelphia *Press:*

"The family of Governor Johnson are here. They were most shamefully treated by the rebels on the way to Nashville. And, although they were sent out by the rebel authorities, under a flag of truce, they were arrested at Murfreesboro', by the guerrillas under Forest, kept under guard all night, in a room without fire, and next day marched back to Tullahoma, a distance of more than thirty miles, and after being detained there for a time, were returned and sent through the lines. The Governor's wife was in bad health, and this exposure and treatment has well nigh killed her. She is now confined to her bed, and my opinion is that she will not recover. With passports, and the authority of Jeff. Davis's government to come out, this sick woman and her helpless children must be arrested, kept in the cold, starved and insulted, and marched to and fro upon the road, because Governor Johnson is not loyal to the hell-born and hell-bound Southern Confederacy! There is not among them even the honor common to thieves. One branch of this bogus government won't respect what another orders."

THE HORRORS OF SOUTHERN INSTITUTIONS.

Under this head the Troy *Times* prints a letter from Mary F. Clark, in support of the statements of General Butler, as to the horrors of Southern society. The *Times* vouches for Mrs. Clark, whose position and character afford sufficient guaranty of her truthfulness. We condense the following statement from her letter :

"I once resided in South Carolina ; returned to my Northern home but two years before the present rebellion. I was governess for six years in the family of the son of ex-Governor Richardson. While there, I was told by Colonel Richardson's own white daughters all I know of the degredation occasioned by slavery. I desired to tell its most degrading features to those whom I have so often heard advocating a continuance of negro slavery ; but I dared not, for the facts seemed too indelicate for a female to publish. But, sir, these are remarkable times ; and should I hold my peace, even the very stones would cry out; for *slavery is a wrong* to the planter's slave and to the planter's daughters."

Referring to Gen. Butler's statement, that a judge of New Orleans debauched his daughter, and then married her to a slave, she says :

"I wish to state that it is the custom of the South Carolina aristocracy for fathers to have criminal intercourse with their own daughters. Col. Richardson had four beautiful daughters, two of whom yielded to his hellish persuasions. The third daughter had for four years refused to listen to the base propositions of her father. He hunted her from room to room, until in very anguish of spirit she came to my room, and hid her face in my lap, and told me all her awful trial. I could not believe the child ; but she told me it was true—that her father gave her no peace. He seemed determined to gratify his hellish lust. He would come to her bedside when she was suffering from sick headache, and attempt to take improper liberties with her person. She begged me to come and sit with her in her room whenever she was confined to her bed, because she was afraid of her own father, who had ruined two of her sisters. She said that one day her cousin Camilla came to visit there. She told her cousin how her father had behaved for the four years past toward her, hoping her cousin Camilla would strengthen her. But Camilla had been ruined by her own father, years before, when she was young, and dared not be woman enough to refuse her father anything he might wish. Her advice to her cousin Mary was this, ' Die before you yield.'

" This is the effect of the institution of slavery. Some may say they cannot see how slavery is responsible for these family evils of which Gen. Butler speaks, and of which I affirm. The secret is just here : from very infancy the planters' sons are gratified in everything they desire. I could tell you some startling facts of the boyhood of these planters' sons,—facts communicated by Col. Richardson's own white daughters—but I forbear. From youth to manhood they go on gratifying every lust, simply because the institution of human bondage puts it in their power to do so ; when they become fathers of black and white children, all must be sacrificed to their overgrown lust. Shall not the prayers of the fair daughters of South Carolina be heeded ? Shall not this evil, slavery, be rooted from our land ? "

OFFICIAL REPORT OF DR. H. R. WIRTZ, OF THE BURNING OF HOSPITALS AND BRUTAL TREATMENT BY THE REBELS.

The following has been forwarded to the headquarters of the army here :

MEDICAL DIRECTOR'S OFFICE, }
Holly Springs, Miss., Dec. 30, 1862. }

SIR :—I have the honor to report that I remained behind the advance of the army for the purpose of establishing a large general hospital at Holly Springs. I took a building that had been built for an armory by the Confederates, consisting of six large rooms, each two hundred and fifty feet long, and numerous outhouses, and after three weeks incessant labor, in which I was greatly assisted by Surgeon Powers, of the 7th Missouri,

I had everything prepared for the accommodation of two thousand men.

The acting medical purveyor of the Southern portion of the department had been ordered to bring all his supplies to this hospital, which he did; and on the morning of the 20th of December one of the most completely finished hospitals in the army was ready to receive its sick. On that morning the town of Holly Springs was taken by the Confederate forces under Gen. Van Dorn. As soon as I discovered the enemy were in possession of the town I repaired to the headquarters of the rebel General, near the town, and made a formal request that the armory hospital should not be burnt, entering my solemn protest on the subject, as the Confederates had already set fire to a railroad depot and a commissary store house, and had declared their intention to destroy all the houses and other buildings occupied by our troops. I received the assurance by Gen. Van Dorn's Adjutant that the armory hospital should not be burnt, but that it would not be protected by a guard. Satisfied with this I returned to my quarters, but had not been there an hour when I was informed that the building was in flames, and thus *this fine structure with 2000 bunks, an immense lot of drugs and surgical apparatus, thousands of blankets, sheets and bed sacks, was soon in ashes.* This proceeding, in violation of an express promise and all rules of civilized warfare, is an evidence of the barbarity and want of principle in the Confederate officers. But this is not all. *An attempt was made to destroy the general hospital located in the main square, and which at the time, contained over five hundred sick.* A quantity of ordnance stores had been deposited in the building in the next block to the hospital, and by the order of Gen. Van Dorn, as stated by the officer who had charge of the matter, the barrels of powder and boxes containing shell and cartridges, were taken out and piled up nearly in front of the hospital and set fire to. Two medical officers protested against this wanton act, but their requests were treated with contempt, and before there was time to remove the sick, the walls and windows of the hospital were riddled with flying balls and shell, and finally a terrific explosion took place which shook the entire building, destroying almost every window and door in the establishment, wounding about twenty men, and creating a scene of the wildest confusion. A large number of buildings on the public square took fire from the explosion, and it was only by the utmost efforts, that the hospital was preserved as a shelter for the men in the night air, together with the medical officers who assisted me in taking care of the sick and wounded on that trying day.

3

I thought the rebels had now done us all the harm in their power, but to injury, insult was to be added, in a manner I hope never to witness again. A rebel cavalry officer named Brewster, who stated that he had been detailed by Van Dorn to march off sick men that had not been paroled, collected together, pistol in hand, 150 sick soldiers, forced them to rise from their beds and fall in line, threatening to shoot the medical officer who expostulated with him, and actually made the poor fellows, suffering from typhoid fever and pneumonia, start with him on the road. The men fell down in the street, and had to rise again for fear of being shot, when they were so weak that the slightest motion was agony. On being importuned if there was anything in the name of humanity that could be done to induce him to cease his brutal proceedings, he finally consented to let them alone on a recognition paper, signed by all the surgeons, representing that the men were too sick to walk, and their removal was an impossibility.

(Signed)　　　　　　　　H. R. WIRTZ,
Surgeon U. S. Army and Medical Director 13th Army Corps.

THE MURDER OF NEGRO TEAMSTERS AT MURFREESBORO, BY ORDER OF THE REBEL GEN. BRAGG.

The wanton murder near Murfreesboro, of 20 negro teamsters, who were in the service of the Unionists, appears to be taken as a matter of course by the advocates of the South in this country. We must presume that they know their friends, and see no reason to be surprised. And yet there are circumstances in this case which should make them anxious for a reputation with which they have so far involved their own. These negroes were not killed in the pursuit of any military purpose. They were not in the battle-field; they were not making armed resistance. They were on the turnpike-road, driving their wagons, when the Confederate party came up. The train which they were conducting was captured, and it was after that object had been gained that the negroes were taken out and shot in cold blood.

It is important to notice that this butchery was perpetrated, not in some corner of Secessia, by agents out of the reach of authority or public opinion; it was the work of officers of the great Confederate army of the West, under the orders of Gen. Bragg. There was nothing in the attitude of the negroes to make a sudden resolution necessary; we must, therefore, assume that their murder was the effect of a previous determination.

We forbear to anticipate the apologies that may be offered for this atrocious slaughter of men who had committed no crime to deserve death. Travelers who have visited the slave States say that if ever England should recognized the South, and come into close intimacy with its people, we shall all be astounded at the character of those whom we have chosen to patronize. It seems that we have not to wait for that contingency. The inevitable hour when the true issues of this war were to be disclosed has come, and the South unfurls the black flag—its own flag—accordingly.—*Daily News, Jan.* 20, 1862.

MURDER OF NEGRO SERVANTS, IN A HOSPITAL BOAT.

After the battle of Stone River, or Murfreesboro, a Federal hospital boat, when conveying the wounded, and bearing the customary flag indicating its object, was fired upon and boarded by the rebels. Some fifteen negroes employed as servants on board the boat were killed. Others endeavoring to escape, were shot in the water while clinging to the sides of the boat. This inhuman treatment was not the work of guerrillas, for whose actions the rebel authorities might endeavor to excuse themselves, but was done by soldiers under the command of a Colonel Wade. General Wheeler's Adjutant General was among the officers present. This Wheeler was promoted for the raid of which the attack on the hospital boat and murder of the negroes was the principal feature.

These facts were made known in a private letter from the Headquarters of the Fourteenth Army Corps, near Murfreesboro, and published in the *New York Evening Post, March* 11, 1863.

HOW THE REBEL SOLDIERS TREAT OUR DEAD AND WOUNDED.—GEN. SILL.

After every battle with the rebels, all accounts agree as to the diabolical practices committed by their soldiers upon our dead and wounded who fall into their hands. Every species of cruelty and malignity is manifested by our enemy towards these unfortunates, which the fortunes of war have placed at their disposal. Of their barbarities on the bodies of the

Union soldiers who fell at the first battle of Bull Run, we have elsewhere spoken. In North Carolina they committed the vilest outrages upon the bodies of those who fell in the expedition to Goldsboro. It cannot, therefore, be asserted that guerrillas, or camp followers, or some particular company of their semi-civilized poor whites, or the "savage Texans" committed these barbarities. The same hellish propensities prevail every where where the institution of slavery exists. Cruelty, brutality, ferocity and inhumanity are the natural offsprings of slavery. It gives rise to, and matures these demoniacal passions, and a civil war furnishes these human devils with the means of gratifying their propensities.

It was stated some time since that the rebels had ordered the body of General Sill, who was killed at Murfreesboro', to be buried with military honors. This was afterwards denied, and we now find in the Nashville *Union* a letter from Surgeon Bowman of the twenty-seventh Illinois volunteers upon the subject, which we quote :

" CAMP ON STONE RIVER, SOUTH OF MURFREESBORO, TENN.,)
JANUARY 20, 1863.)

" *Editor of the Nashville Union:*

" In your issue of the 17th instant, in your editorial under the head of ' A Perfidious People,' in speaking of atrocities by the rebels, you say : ' The dead body of General Sill, whom barbarians would have admired for his chivalrous courage, was stripped on the field of battle. The subsequent honor of a military burial by the enemy was the smallest reparation they could make for this fiendish barbarism. The truth of history compels me to state that the inference that General Sill was buried by the rebels with military honors is not correct. They did not bury him at all, whatever they may have ordered done. I was taken prisoner while attending to our wounded on the 31st ultimo. The enemy charged valiantly upon our extemporized field hospital, where we had up four red flags, fired a volley into us, and then took all prisoners who could be moved. My colonel, F. A. Harrington, of the twenty-seventh Illinois, was very severely wounded. We were taken to Murfreesboro on the afternoon of the 31st. Colonel H. died on the evening of the next day. On the morning of the 2d inst. I procured an order for an extra fine coffin, same as General Sill's was. Found the undertaker with no lumber but green oak and poplar, and but little of that, and beseiged by a crowd of importunate applicants for coffins, boxes, anything in which to bury their dead friends. I laid off my coat, and with the help of a negro, completed a rough coffin, the best the place afforded, and same as General Sill's. I procured the same hearse and driver, so as to bury my friend beside General Sill. The driver took us to the spot where he had left the body of General Sill. We found it in the fence corner unburied, no grave dug, and no detail for that purpose. It was too late in the day (Friday January 2d,) to go back to town to make arrangements. So, after borrowing some tools, which we procured only by energetic representations to the rebels, we dug a grave large enough to contain both coffins ; and with a feeling of sadness, to which language cannot do justice, we lowered them to their resting place, side by side, and heaped the earth over them, putting up the head-board I had prepared with my own hands.''

A correspondent of the Boston *Traveller* says :

" It will be remembered that at Whitehall some of our dead were not interred, the rebel sharp-shooters picking off the men who went for them, bearing the hospital flag. It has been found that all such had been completely stripped of their clothing ; some of them had been considerably mutilated, while many had been so slightly covered with earth that unclean animals had partially exhumed and still further mutilated them. And this was done, or permitted to be done, by persons who are very fond of appealing to the Divine Judge for the rectitude of their intentions, and who are tiring the ears of the nations with their complaints of cruelty and barbarism of their antagonists.''

To the same effect as the above are the reports from the field of Murfreesboro, where Bragg himself violated all decency and humanity. He violated his own flag of truce, robbed his prisoners of their blankets and overcoats, encouraged the plunder of both officers and men who were captured by him, and approved almost every other act of which a fiend can be supposed to be capable. A correspondent of the Cincinnati *Commercial* says :

" The body of General Sill, and those of other officers and privates slain in the battle of Stone river, which fell into their hands, were barbarously plundered, and captive officers were deprived of their personal property.

" Surgeons, who were sacred, not only by the laws of war, but by specific agreement with the rebel authorities, from the usual disposition of prisoners, have been robbed of everything they possessed, except the clothing they wore while in actual custody.

" Dr. Freeman, Assistant Surgeon of the one hundred and fourth Illinois, complains in writing that his horse, equipments, wearing apparel, &c., and those of Dr. Zipperler, of the one hundred and eighth Ohio, were taken by Morgan's men, while the complainants were dressing the wounds of friends and foes, and that when complaint was made to Morgan he would not make restitution. And so on for quantity.

"These rebel people seem more perfidious than Spartans. They regard none of the obligations of honor which bind the rest of mankind. They take oaths but to violate them ; give pledges of the most solemn character that they may escape custody, to deceive those who credited their representations. They prove themselves a race of Cretans as well as Spartans, in their disposition to steal and violate their pledges of honor. If the ignorant only were guilty, there would be hope for them, but the most flagrant acts of infamy are done and encouraged by leading people."

From other fields we have the same reports of inhumanity. In Tennessee and Mississippi gangs of guerrillas everywhere haunt our outposts, murdering in cold blood the innocent and unwary ; digging from their graves, and stripping of the clothing, the bodies of all within their reach ; heaping alike upon the living and the dead, indignities such as even Attalla would have blushed to commit ; and yet there are men, all over the North, living in the midst of schools and churches and all the influence of Christian culture and enlightenment, who uphold the cause which depends for success upon such infernal resources, and who, false to nature and to nurture, desire the erection, on the ruins of the Republic, of a nationality embodying as its vital principle the barbarism out of which alone atrocities so savage and inhuman could proceed !

A dispatch from Murfreesboro, dated December 31, says :

" The enemy during yesterday harassed our rear with their cavalry, and captured some of our wounded men near Nolinsville. Rebel guerrilla bands attacked and burned our army wagons, ambulances, etc., and acted most outrageously, throwing the sick and wounded into the roads to die.

Major Slemmer and Captain King, who were being conveyed away wounded from the battle-field in an ambulance, were captured by the rebels, taken four miles away, and then paroled and thrown out on the road." *Harper's Weekly.*

PROPOSAL OF A REBEL OFFICER TO HANG UNION PRISONERS.

Among the prisoners recently captured by General John McNeil, in Southeast Missouri, and since sent to St. Louis, is a Captain R. T. Sickels, who was rebel Provost-Marshal of Bloomfield, Mo. On the person of Sickels was found a letter instructing him summarily to hang certain persons, in order to save expense, and to prevent them from demoralizing the rebel public sentiment! .The following is the infamous letter:

"OFFICE PROVOST-MARSHAL,
POCAHONTAS, ARK., January 15, 1863. }

" *Captain R. T. Sickels :*

" Dear Sir : The prisoner you sent up has been received, and has been duly forwarded.

" In future you will deal summarily with those men who are guilty of criminal offences, for when they are sent up to headquarters they are an expense, without being any benefit to public sentiment. Captain McKie says it would be better to have them hung than to put ourselves to any further trouble.   Yours, &c.,

" M. H. KIBLEE,

" Captain, Provost Marshal, Randolph Co., Ark."

The guerrilla captain on whom the above precious document was found is now in a United States military prison. There are proofs that he did not fail to comply with the execrable instructions given him.

HORRID PROPOSAL OF THE REBEL MILITARY COMMANDER OF ARIZONA, COLONEL BAYLOR, TO ENTRAP AND MURDER A WHOLE TRIBE OF INDIANS.

The following extract from the *New Orleans Delta* tells its own story :

We are indebted to Captain Longley, of the 1st Texas Cavalry, for the following choice contributions to the history of the rebellion, taken from Texas papers. " Col." Baylor's position, as a rebel alone, entitles him to the attention of the *Delta*. Personally, he is just such a scoundrel as his official acts proclaim him. It is a very significant commentary on the character of the rebellion that such a notorious bully, blackguard, and horse-thief, should be entrusted with important duties in the service of the Richmond oligarchy. Texas needs no information concerning him.

The civilized world cannot read the extract given below—cut from a Houston paper—without some hardly favorable reflections on the nature of the insurrection, its leaders and agents. Baylor has borne for some time a considerable reputation as an Indian fighter, from the fact that by just such a piece of abominable treachery as he delegates to " Capt." Helm, in the order here published, he managed to massacre a large number of Indians, principally women and children, some time since, and was enabled in this way to make a magnificent display of scalps as the trophies of his heroism. The order of Capt. Helm was, of course, not sent to the papers, but was published at a later day by "Gen." Sibley, with comments.

The "General" took occasion also to send the order to Richmond, and as a return for the notice bestowed upon him, Baylor undertakes in a later publication, given here also, to ventilate the character of Sibley. It is not likely that he much misrepresents the notorious Sibley, whose skedaddling exploits in the rebel service since he turned traitor and deserted the United States army, where he held a major's commission, are very well known to the public. They are *par nobile fratrum*, and not likely to say anything too bad of each other. Any criticism on Baylor's production would be time wasted. Rascality and cowardice united had never a more damning exposition. There can be no question whatever as to the authenticity of the documents:

"HEADQUARTERS SECOND REGIMENT T. M. R., }
MESILLA, March 20, 1862. }

"*Captain Helm, Commanding Arizona Guards:*

SIR: I learn from Lieutenant Colonel Jackson that the Indians have been in your post, for the purpose of making a treaty. *The congress of the Confederate States has passed a law declaring extermination to all hostile Indians. You will therefore use all possible means to pursuade the Apaches, or any other tribes, to come in for making peace ; and, when you get them together, kill all the grown Indians, and take the children prisoners, and sell them to defray the expenses of killing the Indians.*

Buy whiskey and such other goods as may be necessary for the Indians, and I will order vouchers given to cover the amount expended.

Leave nothing undone to insure success, and have a sufficient number of men around to allow no Indians to escape. Say nothing about your orders until the time arrives, and be cautious how you let the Mexicans know it. If you can't trust them, send to Captain Aycock at this place, and he will send thirty men from his company. Better use the Mexicans, if they can be trusted, as bringing troops from here might excite suspicion with the Indians.

To your judgment I entrust this important matter, and look for success against these cursed pests who have already murdered over one hundred men in this Territory. JOHN R. BAYLOR,
Col. Commanding 2d Regt. T. M. R."

The infamous Baylor, on learning that Gen. Sibley had sent his order to massacre the Indians to Jeff. Davis, had the impudence to come out with a defence of his conduct in the columns of the San Antonio (Texas) papers, which, it appears, were horrified with the proposal of Baylor. The ruffian Colonel does not deny the allegation, but attempts to palliate his conduct. "There is no question," he says "about the genuineness of my order. I issued it, and meant precisely what I said; and if I am so fortunate as to return to Arizona, *I intend to get rid of the Indians any way I can.*"

Baylor is quite severe upon Gen. Sibley for being so shocked with his order. He calls him "an infamous coward, and a disgrace to the Confederate army;" denounces him "for all that is mean and worthless," and accuses him with having "doubled himself up in an ambulance during the battle of Valverde, and hoisted a hospital flag on it for his protection." He furthermore thinks that Sibley's horror at the proposed massacre was less than his grief at the probable waste of the whiskey which Baylor intended to use to inveigle the poor, confiding Indians. A precious set of scoundrels, these Texan officers! Yet fair specimens of the "Southern Chivalry."

HORRID TREATMENT AND MURDER OF NEGRO BOYS AND COOKS.

Shocking brutalities were committed upon a number of negroes who were employed as waiters and cooks, upon several Union steamboats on the Cumberland river. These boats, five in number, which were transporting commissary stores and wounded soldiers, were taken and burnt by the rebels at Harpeth Shoals. The transports, were, of course, fair objects for capture; but the hospital boats received no more consideration than though they had been war vessels. The officers and men were subjected to the greatest indignities, and after being robbed of their clothes were placed on shore and paroled. But for the poor negroes no kind of cruelty was deemed too severe by their captors. "*These unarmed and defenceless men were stripped of their clothing, tied to trees,* and *cowhided.*" They were then put ashore and left to perish on the uninhabited banks of the river, where escape was impossible. Such barbarities are enough to make one lose all faith in human nature. It is proper to remark that these brutalities were committed under the eye of the rebel Brigadier-General Forrest. —*New York Illustrated News, Feb.* 7, 1863.

Fuller particulars of this cold-blooded barbarity were published in the

New Albany (Indiana) *Ledger,* of the 20th of January, 1863. They are as follows :

" The most atrocious and cold-blooded affair of the present war is the shooting of some eighteen of the negro cabin boys and cooks on the steamers lately captured at Harpeth Shoals. These men and boys were tied and taken to an open field near the Shoals, and deliberately shot down in cold blood. Two of the negro servants on the Sidell got in between the wheel and stern of the boat, and let themselves down into the water, holding on to the rudder. They were discovered by the rebels, and several soldiers were ordered into a skiff, and rowing close up to the unfortunate negroes, discharged the contents of their muskets at them, literally blowing their heads into atoms.

" The damnable villany of such cold-blooded murder cannot but fill every heart with the fiercest indignation, and will beget measures of the bloodiest retaliation.

" The life of the chambermaid of the Trio was saved by Mr. Hurley, the clerk, claiming her as his slave, whom he was removing to Kentucky. And even with this pretext he had the greatest difficulty in saving her from death at the hands of the bloody-minded commander of the rebels, Colonel Wade. We hope this scoundrel may be captured, and if he is, quartering would be a slight penalty for his villanous murder of these unoffending negroes. His acts of barbarity have scarcely an equal, even in the history of the most savage warfare."

CONTRABANDS DRIVEN SOUTH OR SHOT.

A correspondent from Murfreesboro writes :

" All contrabands captured by the rebels on the Federal wagon-trains are immediately shot. Twenty thus killed are lying on the Murfreesboro Pike."

UNIONISTS IN MISSISSIPPI HUNTED DOWN BY BLOOD-HOUNDS, AND THEIR DWELLINGS BURNED.—OFFICIAL REPORT OF THESE BARBARITIES.

Repeated statements have been made that in various parts of the rebellious States, blood-hounds, (which are kept by slave-owners to hunt down and recapture runaway slaves) were employed to hunt down Unionists who had fled to the deep recesses of the mountain, swamps and forests, to escape the conscription, or for protection from the cruelties of the rebel officers. Narratives of these have, from time to time, appeared in our public journals. The following appeared in the Washington papers, to which, as well as to the New York papers, it was officially communicated on the 5th of March, 1863.

HEADQUARTERS DISTRICT OF CORINTH, }
MISSISSIPPI, Jan. 24, 1863. }

Captain—I have the honor to submit a few of the outrages committed upon citizens of Alabama by the confederate troops. While all their leaders, from the President down, are boasting of their carrying on this war in accordance with the laws that govern nations in such cases, and are charging upon our troops all kinds of depredations and outrages, I think a few simple facts might put them to blush, and make those parties and our press and people who are seconding the efforts of Davis to cast a stigma on us, ashamed of the work they are doing. I will state merely what I know to be true. Abe Canadi and Mr. Mitchel were hung two weeks ago for being Union men. They lived on Hacklebon settlement, Marion county, Alabama. Mr. Hallwork and his daughter, of the same county, were both shot for the same cause ; the latter was instantly killed ; the former is still alive, but will probably die. *Peter Lewis and three of his neighbors were hunted down by one hundred bloodhounds and captured.*

The houses of Messrs. Palmer, Welsby, Williams and the three neighbors, and of some thirty others, were burned over their heads. The women and children were turned out of doors, and the community was notified that if they allowed them to go into their houses, or fed or harbored them in any manner, they would be served in the same manner.

Mr. Peterson, living at the head of Bull Mountain, was shot.

I am now feeding some hundred of these families, who, with their wives and children, some grey haired men, and even cripples on crutches, were driven out and found their way here through the woods and by-ways without food or shelter. All this was done for the simple reason that they were Union men, or that they had brothers or relations in our army.

The statements of these people are almost beyond belief, did we not have the evidence before us. I am informed by them that there are hundreds of loyal men and women in the woods of Alabama waiting for an opportunity to escape.

I am, very respectfully, your obedient servant,

G. M. DODGE, Brig. Gen.

Capt. R. M. Sawyer, A. A. G., Memphis.

SUFFERINGS OF LOYALISTS IN WEST VIRGINIA.

Dr. Watson, of the Senate of Western Virginia, in a communication to the Wheeling *Intelligencer*, in which he corrects' certain misstatements of a secession organ of that city, gives some very interesting information as to the sufferings experienced by many of the citizens of that state who have fallen into the hands of the rebels. Dr. Watson mentions cases of the grossest cruelty to men, women and children, who have been seized and carried into captivity. Among others, he names the case of a Mrs. Spiggott, sister of the newly-elected United States senator. Judge Bowden, who, with her four children, is now imprisoned in a dungeon in Richmond, for no crime in the world save her unconquerable attachment to the Union. Another case is that of a Mr. Mannocks, of Williamsburg, who was dragged from his home—his family left to want—and sent to Salisbury, N. C., and is now there in a filthy cell. This man was one of the most inoffensive citizens in the state, and never harmed or wronged any one, loyal or disloyal. The case of Mr. Mannocks is the case also of a Mr. Morrison, on old man seventy years of age, taken from near Elizabeth City more than a year ago, and ever since confined in prison.

Dr. Watson, with a view to the prevention of such barbarous outrages in the future, and for the relief of present sufferers, lately introduced in the state Senate the following resolutions, which were immediately passed, without a dissenting voice :

Whereas, It is represented to the General Assembly that the rebel authorities in Virginia have arrested and now have confined in prison many citizens, civilians and non-combatants, including men, women and children, on the pretence of their disloyalty to the pretended Southern Confederacy ; therefore, it is

Resolved, By the General Assembly that the President of the United States be and he is hereby respectfully requested to order commanding officers in this state to retaliate, by arresting or causing to be arrested such number of known adherents or sympathizers with the pretended Confederacy as, in his opinion, may be expedient, to be held in close confinement, as hostages, and subjected in all respects, as nearly as may be, to the same treatment which is imposed upon loyal citizens by the said pretended government; and to make such other or further order as in his opinion shall be necessary to effect the release of such citizens as are now, or may hereafter, be so arrested and confined by the rebel authority.

CRUELTIES OF THE SOUTHERN WOMEN.

General Butler was severely censured by the apologists of secession for his celebration " women order." But the revelations which the war is making of the ferocity of female secessionists are fast dissipating any rose-water notions people may have entertained as to the justice of that order. A gentleman who recently fell in with an intelligent Illinois officer gives the following as the result of his observations and experience among the women of the rebel states :

" The men are brave and bitter ; the southern women ten-fold worse than the men. He says in a recent battle, when our men were compelled to charge through a small town in pursuit of the rebels, they were shot down by women and girls, armed with revolvers and shot-guns, from windows and crevices in the buildings which lined the street. Of course our troops returned the fire, but, with a foe in front, but little could be done to dislodge these female desperadoes. Exasperated by the galling fire from these buildings, the torch was applied and the town destroyed. Was it wrong ? If so, the natural instinct of self-preservation should be rooted out of the army. At another time, this captain said his regiment was marching through the country in Tennessee, and passing near a planter's house, five women were noticed standing near the gate. He took no notice of them. The right division of his company had passed them ; as the left devision came opposite, these five women drew revolvers and fired into the ranks, killing two men instantly, and mortally wounding another. Impulsively our soldiers, without orders, returned the fire, killing four of the women and severely wounding the fifth. General Ross (I think) commanded the devision, and hearing the firing, galloped up to learn the cause. He was disposed to censure the captain for allowing his troops to fire at women. The captain pleaded first, that the firing was done without his knowledge or order, and second that he could not punish his men for firing upon women when they unsex themselves by deliberately murdering Union soldiers. He would leave the service first. So long as women behave as women should, he would do what he could to protect them ; but when they assume the place of men and the character of combatants, he would treat them as such, and justify his men in so doing."—*New York Evening Post.*

A SOUTHERN WOMAN DESIRES TO DANCE IN THE BLOOD OF A UNION SOLDIER.—In accounts given by Commissary Packham, of Piatt's Zouaves, 34th regiment, Ohio volunteers, printed elsewhere, is a notice of a Mrs.

Gilkinson, to whose house, in Western Virginia, several Federal prisoners were taken by their rebel captors and confined during the night. In the morning there was a difference of opinion as to the disposal of the prisoners. Some wished to send them to Richmond, others to Logan Court House, the head-quarters of the rebel troops, while others proposed to kill them on the spot. The Virginia lady, Mrs. Gilkinson, writes Commissary Packham, "to the eternal disgrace of Southern female fiends, *wished one of the prisoners to be killed on her own porch, so that she could dance in his blood!!"—Harper's Weekly.*

TREATMENT OF THE QUAKERS IN NORTH CAROLINA.

Extract of a letter from Philadelphia to the New York Tribune, dated Aug. 6, 1863.—"The leading particulars of one of the most remarkable events in this war have just been communicated to me. You know that many of the Society of Friends have long resided in North Carolina, and that a fundamental article of their faith is a refusal to take up arms under any circumstances whatever. In the early stages of the rebellion the rebel powers of North Carolina, well knowing their peaceful principles, permitted them to pass unmolested, though known to be unconditional Union men. But as time went on, disaster to the rebellion succeeded to disaster, men were captured, killed or disabled to so fearful an extent, that every one out of the army must be brought into it.

Early this year the conscription fell upon the Friends. In one neighborhood, some twelve of them were drafted. In accordance with their well-known principles, they refused to join the army. But everywhere the reign of terror prevailed, and they were forced into the ranks. Here muskets were given to them, but every man of them refused even to touch the weapons. Every conceivable insult and outrage was heaped upon them; they were tied up, starved and whipped. Still they remained firm to their conscientious convictions, and refused to fight. Finally, the muskets were actually strapped to their bodies.

One of these Friends was singled out as especially obnoxious, and was whipped unmercifully. The officer in charge was lawless and brutal, and on one occasion ordered him to be shot as an example to others. He called out a file of men to shoot him. While his executioners were drawn up before him, standing within twelve feet of their victim, the latter, raising his eyes to heaven, and elevating his hands, cried out in a loud voice: "Father, forgive them; they know not what they do." Instantly came the order to fire. But instead of obeying it, the men dropped their muskets and refused, declaring that they could not kill such a man.

This refusal so enraged the officer that he knocked his victim down in the road, and then strove repeatedly to trample him to death under his horse's feet. But the animal persistently refused to even step over his prostrate body. In the end, they were marched with the rebel army to Gettysburg. In that battle they remained entirely passive, fired no shots, and in God alone trusted for preservation. Very early in the action the officer referred to was killed. The Friends, all unhurt, were taken prisoners and sent to Fort Delaware. Here, by accident, it became known in this city that several Friends were among the captured, and two members of the Society went down to inquire into the circumstances, but they were refused permission to see them. They went immediately to Washington, and there obtained an order for their discharge, conditioned on their taking an affirmation of their allegiance. This opened the prison door. The affirmation made, these martyrs for conscience sake were released, and are now here.''

TREATMENT OF PRISONERS TAKEN AT CHANCELLORSVILLE AND OTHER PLACES.

A correspondent of the Springfield (Mass.) *Republican*, who was taken prisoner at Chancellorsville and sent to Richmond, gives the follow ing account of rebel hospitality : ·

" I have been among Italian brigands, and Greek pirates, and Bedouin Arabs, but for making a clean thing of the robbing business, commend me to the Confederate States of America, so styled. They descend to the minutiæ of the profession in a way that should be instructive to all novices in the art. Nothing is too small to escape their microscopic rapacity. No article of apparel is sacred from their omnivorous clutches ; no crumb of provision but their acute olfactories will smell it out. They ransacked our haversacks, and confiscated the little rations of sugar we happened to have therein as contraband of war. They stripped the canteens from the shoulders of the thirsty soldiers, and are sending them off on a long march, to suffer no small inconvenience from this privation. They are taking away all our blankets, without which these cold nights will be almost insupportable till we can obtain a new supply. They picked our pockets of the few stray envelopes and sheets and half sheets of writing paper we chanced to possess ; and this, be it understood, not as a precaution to pre vent our writing in prison. There is no regulation to prevent that, no prohibition of our sending out and purchasing all the paper we wished. But it is just a specimen of the scale on which they conduct business.

" And in another way the official proceedings of this chivalrous Confederacy are just about as small. A system of petty annoyance and oppression, on the smallest possible scale, has been uniformly observed in reference to the Union prisoners in their hands. When they wished to remove the hundred or so Federal officers by rail from Guinney's Station to Richmond, they ordered us to prepare to move at 3 p. m., kept us standing in ranks in a pouring rain for several hours, then marched us half a mile to the cars, and kept us waiting there, the rain still pouring furiously upon us, till half-past 10 p. m., when they marched us back to our flooded camps again, with orders to be in readiness at a moment's notice, two or three hours hence, or any time during the night.

" Losing all our rest that night, and wandering about, forlorn and dripping, we heard nothing more of moving till the next afternoon about four o'clock, when we were put through the same process of waiting, and the second time kicked our heels about the station in the deep mud till seven or eight p. m., when we were ordered back to camp again, but afterward did get aboard and spend the night in the box cars (awfully dirty), although we did not move till noon the third day. All this, of course, as a mere annoyance to us, and to make a display of their power, as nothing could be easier than to know when there was a train for us. And of a piece with this is the order given to the sentinels here to prevent us from looking out of the windows of the Libby, on pain of being fired upon. In the same style is pretty much the whole of the Confederate behavior to us-ward.

Lieut. Kenyon, of the 28th N. Y. volunteers, lately returned from Richmond, tells a similar account of cruelties. Their food, until they reached Richmond, would hardly sustain life. " Upon our march," says Lieut. Kenyon, " away from Richmond, a variety of cruelties and annoyances were inflicted upon the paroled men by the rebel guard. They were made to march nine miles without a minute's halt, and when the men fell down from absolute exhaustion, they were forced up and into the ranks at the point of the bayonet, being assailed with words of the coarsest abuse. General officers and privates were treated alike in this respect ; and all this was done, too, when a railway train almost empty was accompanying the march."

" While passing through Petersburg they were assailed by the residents of the place with bad language, and *even ladies pressed forward to insult the prisoners.* In this respect Petersburg was far more demonstrative than Richmond."—*New York Evening Post.*

FEDERAL PRISONERS BAYONETED AT BALL'S BLUFF.—The Rev. Mr. Anghey, relates some of the barbarities towards the Union soldiers taken in battle which almost surpass belief. All the Southern accounts of the battle of Leesburg, (which we call the battle of Ball's Bluff,) he says concur in one particular, which is, that " when the Federal troops retreated to the river, after being overpowered by superior numbers, and had thrown down their arms, calling for quarter, no mercy was shown them. *Hundreds were bayoneted*, or forced into the river and drowned. The rebels clubbed their guns, and dashed out the brains of many while kneeling at their feet and imploring mercy. I saw one ruffian who boasted that he had bayoneted seven Yankee prisoners captured on that occasion."

HORRORS OF THE KNOXVILLE (TENN.) JAIL.

An officer of the forty-fourth Ohio regiment, who has just been released from the Knoxville (Tenn.) jail, reports that there is a strong, outspoken Union sentiment at Knoxville. The jail there, is filled with loyal citizens of Tennessee, who are treated with all possible harshness and cruelty, and are kept in a most loathsome manner. The jail is so crowded that the prisoners are compelled to take turns in sleeping. There are in it six cages about ten feet square. In each of which there are confined from five to seven prisoners—generally those who are the strongest friends of the old Union. In addition to these, the rebels have in jail three federal officers, in chains. They are Captain Harris, of the third Tennessee cavalry, Captain Deacon, of the second Tennessee infantry, and Lieutenant Rodgers, of the first Tennessee cavalry. Captain Harris was once sentenced to death, but his father paid seventy-five thousand dollars to have his sentence commuted to imprisonment for life. The Union women of Knoxville do all they are allowed to do for the relief of the sufferings of the prisoners. The guard of the jail is composed almost entirely of boys, the men having been sent to the field.

THE MURDER OF COLONEL CAMERON.

A few days after the evacuation of Jackson by our forces, Gen. Grant sent two wagon loads of provision back from our front under a flag of truce for the use of our wounded there. The officer in charge was a major of the 2d Illinois cavalry. When within two miles of the town, our men were met by the rebel pickets, who at first would permit them to proceed no further. The major in command refused to deliver the provisions to any other person than the Union surgeon in chrage of our wounded at Jackson, and was finally allowed to enter the town, blindfolded, while Confederate soldiers drove his teams. He found the citizens very much excited, and very indignant about the sacking of the city by our soldiers. They insulted him repeatedly.

While there he heard of the murder of Col. Cameron, of the 47th Illinois, by a party of rebel cavalry. Col. Cameron remained behind our forces after the evacuation of Jackson, to urge stragglers forward. He was alone without any of his command. At the public square a crowd of citizens surrounded him, and commenced heaping violent abuse upon him. He replied to them, kindly and pleasantly, that he was sorry for the existence of the war, and hoped it would soon end, but only in the restoration of the Union. He had a wife and family at home, he said, and he much preferred their company to the army. Finding that he was exciting a good deal of sympathy, a rebel officer marched up and made a breach through the crowd, through which he could pass. Col. Cameron rode off. He had gone but a short distance when a squad of rebel cavalry dashed after him, overtook him, and shot him through the heart. This is the story of an Episcopal Bishop who lives in the city.

MORE REBEL BARBARITIES.

The Columbus (Ky.) *War Eagle* of a recent date gives the following :

" The victim was a Union man, named Jordan Hills, and lived on the Mobile and Ohio Railroad, eighteen miles from Troy. On the 27th of March, Mr. Hills was taken by a party of men claiming to belong to Dawson's band of rebel guerrillas ; he was tied up and whipped, and afterwards gagged, his ears and nose cut off, and three of his fingers amputated and carried away as trophies and souvenirs ! Afterwards, his skull was laid open with a sabre, and his brains scattered and trampled upon by the murderers—and all because he was a Union man, and not a traitor."

The chaplain of a New Jersey regiment in McClellan's army writes :

" The savage barbarity with which rebel soldiers have treated our men who have fallen into their hands as prisoners, has greatly diminished the sympathies with which these captives would be otherwise regarded. But even now they are as well fed as our own men, in some instances even better.

" I command my men to restrain themselves, and not descend to the level of these savages by committing the same atrocities, even in revenge. But when the rebels persist in these outrages, and our government and commanding officers themselves permit them, the wild torrent of revenge may break forth among our soldiers at any moment."

OUR WOUNDED AT CHARLESTON.—THE COLORED SOLDIERS.

Extract of a letter from Morris Island, printed in the New York *Tribune*:

" The Charleston papers, from the 21st to the 24th inst., all say that six hundred and fifty of our killed were buried on the Sunday morning after the assualt. This extraordinary proportion of the killed to the wounded could not have been reached without an indiscriminate murdering of our soldiers, after they had fallen, wounded and helpless.

Our entire loss in killed, wounded and missing, according to official report, was but one thousand five hundred and seventeen ; if six hundred and fifty of that number were buried, as rebel officers and rebel newspapers solemnly assert, it was the most fearful slaughter, considering the numbers engaged, of the war.

One hundred and eight of our wounded are still at Charleston and Columbia. The officers and men of the 54th Massachusetts (colored) will not be given up, nor has it yet been positively ascertained what has become of them.

Unofficial reports say the negroes have been sold into slavery, and that the officers are treated with unmeasured abuses.

Of the latter there is no doubt whatever. I have conversed with several officers who were exchanged on Friday, and they all tell me that the first question asked them was whether they commanded negro troops. If the response was in the negative, they were told it was fortunate for them, for every d—d nigger commander would be hung or shot at sight.

There is but one opinion with regard to the treatment our wounded received in Charleston. It was cruel, shameful, barbarous. Nearly every sentiment of humanity seems to have departed from these South Carolina wretches. The slightest gun-shot wound, which our army surgeons would have soon healed, immediately suggested to these professional butchers the knife, the saw, amputation. and, in this climate, death.

Every opportunity to mutilate the body by amputation was seized upon, and after the operation was performed, the surgeons seemed profoundly indifferent whether a spark of life remained or not. This shameful treatment was not confined to the severely wounded, but nearly all who were so unfortunate as to fall into their hands. "

As it has since been ascertained that the colored soldiers, taken prisoners, had been or would be sold into slavery, the President has ordered that the same number of rebel prisoners be placed at hard labor until the colored soldiers have been liberated, or treated like other prisoners.

UNION WOMEN TAKEN PRISONERS.—THEIR CRUEL TREATMENT.

A number of women, with their children, arrived in Philadelphia, late on Wednesday night, in charge of J. B. Brown, of the Sanitary Commission of Washington. They had been captured from Milroy's command at Winchester, Virginia, and were sent to Richmond as prisoners; most of them belong to Ohio, and were on a visit to their husbands, who were sick. They speak severely of the treatment they received at the hands of the rebels; much of their clothing and money was taken from them. One of them requested to see her husband, who was sick, but was told she could not do it unless he died. Several of them saw their clothes sold at public auction, and on their way to prison they were hooted at by the women and boys of Richmond. Last Sunday the rebels took all their deserters out of prison and armed them. Some of them had been in prison for near two years. Among them were some not more than fourteen years of age, and others from sixty to seventy years old.—*New York Evening Post, July* 10, 1863.

BUTCHERY OF NEGROES IN ALABAMA.

Rev. J. B. Rogers, chaplain of the fourteenth Wisconsin regiment, who has been in charge of the freed blacks at Cairo for some months, confirms a statement which appeared in the papers last fall, of the fiendish barbarity of the rebels in Northern Alabama, which was so monstrous as to be received with incredulity. He says that the rebels actually butchered about a thousand blacks, to prevent them falling into the hands of the Union army. Two hundred were confined in a large building, the building fired, and every one of them burned to death.—*New York Evening Post, April* 25, 1863.